Special

Children

David Hughes

Cover Photograph
Yanina

Born December 13th 1994
Died January 31st 2003

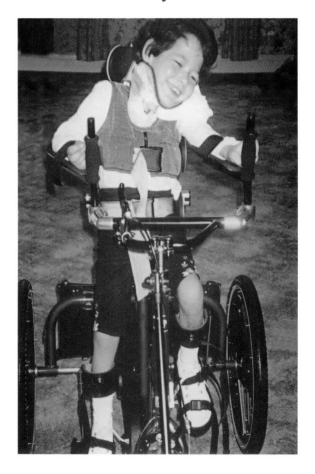

By kind permission of parents Marie and John

Contents

Foreword

Parents have high expectations when their child is born.
All presume that their children will outlive them.
Re-adjustment of these hopes usually occurs for parents of
children with significant disability, and yet their love for
them is undeminished. Indeed these children often seem to
be loved just that little bit more.

This book is very special. David Hughes has sensitively
captured the stories of children and their families and their
courageous response to the challenges which face them.
Each vignette gives us an insight into the happiness as well
as adversity in their lives. I am sure you will be moved by
this narrative.

The hospice in Sunderland that will support these children is
to be called Grace House. The Christian definition of grace
is the pure love which God shows mankind. Perhaps Grace
House is the vehicle by which we can show our care for children and families similar to those so eloquently described in
this book.

Dr Geoff Lawson
Consultant Paediatrician and Clinical Director Child Health
Sunderland Royal Hospital

A Special Prayer

A meeting was held quite far from earth,
it's time again for another birth,
said the angels to the Lord above.

"This special child will need much love.
She may not run or laugh or play,
her thoughts might seem quite far away
in many ways she won't adapt,
and she'll be known as 'handicapped'."

So let's be careful where she's sent,
we want her life to be content.
Please Lord find parents who,
will do a very special job for you.
They will not realise right away,
the leading role they're asked to play,
but with this child sent from above
comes stronger faith and richer love.

Maisie Reilly

David Hughes 2005

First printed in Great Britain 2005 by Digiset Ltd
Published by David Hughes

ISBN: 0-9551067-0-2

Printed by: Digiset Ltd.
                  William Street
                  Felling
                  Gateshead
                  Tyne & Wear
                  NE10 0JP

Acknowledgements

My family & friends, they have tolerated my obsession to write this book.

Every contributor, without whom this book would not exist.

Mrs Karen Maclennan, she accepted my constant changes, revisions and grammatical shortcomings and produced a computer script and disc.

Sunderland Echo, for allowing the reproduction of press reports.

Mr Brian Corker, President Rotary, Chester-le-Street, who generously designed the book cover.

Mrs Peggy Little, Chairperson, Washington Writers, proof reader.

Dr. Geoff Lawson,
Consultant Paediatrician and Clinical Director Child Health
Sunderland Royal Hospital
for the foreword in this book and his encouragement to embark on the project.

Mr Simon Minto and Mr Dave Scott of Digiset.
The print company who provided generous support, advice, greeting cards and books of high quality.

Mr Paul Larkin
Deputy Editor, Sunderland Echo
for his professional assistance and contribution.

Mr Steve McClary, Lasertech. For his generous support.

ALL PROFITS FROM THIS BOOK
WILL BE DONATED
TO
GRACE HOUSE CHILDREN'S
HOSPICE APPEAL

Chapter One

Invitation

"Sorry mate, I've never heard of it."
The workman then shouted to a man up a ladder who was cleaning windows.
"Any idea where Grace House is?"
"Never heard of it. It can't be in this area, we do all the windows."
I returned to the car, they continued cleaning windows. I carried on driving around a huge business complex on the bank of the River Wear, late for a meeting starting ten minutes before. Every inch of parking space was covered by modern, expensive cars, thousands of pounds standing idle all day and I was looking for the office of a charity. Suddenly a shrill voice was shouting "David! David! Over here." I stopped the car to see a lady waving her arms to get my attention, which wasn't difficult considering the deathly silence in the amphitheatre of the circular car park, surrounded by hundreds of windows. Anyone looking down from their office window would be speculating the reason why a young woman was frantically attracting the attention of a white-haired old man who was driving a ten-year-old Volvo.

I'd only met the young lady once before at a very brief meeting. She had an infectious smile and immediately eliminated protocol by using my first name and insisting that I called her Karen. She had the mandatory enthusiasm of a

1

charity fundraiser, and directed me to an empty space, to park my car – I was impressed. "Nice to see you again, David." Her warm greeting was obviously genuine and I followed her to a door that I assumed would lead to Grace House. We climbed dark stairs up to the second floor, turned left and entered an office.

A silky, laughing voice from behind a screen purred: "Hello darling." The voice hadn't changed; she was as beautiful as ever and looked much younger than her age. Kathy Secker and I had known each other for more years than either of us care to remember. She was a star of radio and television, her face constantly featured in the press and magazines and now she was involved with a charity.

I'd first met Kathy more than twenty years ago when she had been contracted to make television commercials for the Co-Op where I was the Retail and Marketing Executive. We didn't meet again until the year 2000 at the launch of my first book, A Journey to Remember at the Beamish Museum in Co. Durham. Although I'd seen her face in the press and on television, our next meeting was by pure chance in 2004.

As a member of a writers' group in Washington, I assisted in raising £250 for the Grace House Appeal and to my surprise it was Kathy who arrived to collect the cheque. In our conversation she asked if I was prepared to help in fundraising. She explained why she, her small team and her army of volunteer fund-raisers and givers, devoted time and energy to finding £5 million pounds to build Grace House Children's Hospice in Sunderland.

She explained the need for another children's hospice in the North East for children with life-threatening illness, that it would be a place for the whole family, but a phrase in the publicity brochure seemed to stay in my mind more than anything else she had said:

"We cannot change the outcome, but we can all help to make the journey just a little bit easier by providing the very best care wherever and whenever it is needed along the way. That is what we believe these special children and their families deserve. That is what Grace House will provide for families throughout the North East."

Could there be anything more worthwhile than helping children in such heart-breaking circumstances?

The task Kathy had embarked upon was monumental. Five million pounds was needed to build, equip and run Grace House for at least its first year.

My experience in fundraising over the past four years was extensive. With my good friend Bill Fish, we had raised thousands of pounds for Marie Curie Cancer Care, Mencap and Orphans in Palestine. We had discovered a world of fundraisers who devote countless hours for their particular charity

I left the Grace House office with a promise to Kathy that I would think about her two requests, - design four greetings cards that could be sold exclusively for the charity and write an inspirational book about the lives of children with life-limiting and life-threatening illness and the affect on their families.

When I mentioned the proposal to friends I was faced with a barrage of negative comments – "That will be a morbid job", "I couldn't do that!", "Do you really want to do such a task at your age?"

I think their comments were a contributing factor in my decision. So many people didn't even want to talk about seriously-ill children and the thought of stories being recorded in a book seemed abhorrent to them.

I understood their feelings. I already filled every day of my life, and I was no longer a young man, but that short phrase in the brochure was so poignant and created many images in my mind of children who could not be cured.

A few days later I picked up the phone and said: "Kathy, I'll help. I'll design your greeting cards and attempt to write a book."

"I knew you would," Kathy replied, with a chuckle in her voice. Little did I know how that decision would affect my life. I would share unbelievable sorrow and heartache, be inspired by stories of devotion and endeavour, but I would begin to look at life in a way that had never entered my head. I would be more thankful than ever at my own good fortune and come to realise the wide gap between children with life-threatening illness, their families and the rest of us.

I was about to embark on a journey into an area of our population of which I was unaware. I would discover what it was really like to be part of the "whole" team caring for children with life-limiting or life-threatening illnesses, in other words, children who could not be cured and were not expected to reach adulthood. Parents, families, teachers, nurses, doctors and many others, all gave love, care, skill and part of their own lives to help children to have as full a life as possible.

This journey would be the most enlightening, inspirational and humbling of my life.

Chapter Two

Birth of a Dream

The first step in my journey would be to find information about the proposed children's hospice. I was entering unknown territory and information would only be obtained by speaking to people. At this stage I had no idea how long my journey of discovery would be or what twists and turns it would take.

Grace House Hospice Appeal and the name of Kathy Secker were becoming synonymous in the Wearside area; rarely did a week go by without her name and face appearing in the local Sunderland newspaper. She was usually featured at a festival, fun run or visiting a local W.I. meeting, all for the same purpose - to accept a donation for her charity appeal. No occasion was too grand or humble, whether a few pounds or many thousands of pounds, she was available and all were treated in the same fashion, with courteous gratitude and a beaming smile.

Who was Kathy Secker? What was Grace House? And how were the two inextricably linked?

Kathy Secker was arguably the best-known media performer in the North of England, from Berwick to Leeds her name and voice were recognised. She appeared regularly on television and radio and was a weekly contributor in a Newcastle newspaper. At Christmas she found time to rehearse and perform in a pantomime, she had a huge base of ardent fans and had been at the pinnacle of her chosen profession for more than twenty five years.

To the general public, her image was of a tall, beautiful, blonde lady with immaculate poise, utmost courtesy and a beaming smile.

Away from the public her beauty, charm and smile remained. In addition she was a shrewd, hardworking lady, knew where she was going, would not be deterred, and would not suffer fools lightly.

A Woman
With A
Mission

Kathy Secker

Over twenty five years' involvement in media work made it inevitable she would be called upon to assist various charities and her very first charity work was in 1978 with Tyne Tees Television. Since then she had opened bazaars, fetes, carnivals and fundraising events too numerous to list.

It began to dawn on Kathy that facilities for children with life-limiting illness were inadequate and for the families of these

8

unfortunate children they were almost non-existent. She decided to do something.

She embarked on a twelve-month research project that was so extensive it would have been daunting to a less determined person. It involved meeting with consultant paediatricians, palliative care specialists, community nurses, social services, special schools, children's charities and families with children who had life limiting conditions. A number of the professionals first approached now form the Project Development Group.

In addition some significant reports were studied, day visits were made to Rachel House in Kinross, Hope House in Oswestry, Butterwick on Teeside and St Oswald's in Newcastle. Not a stone was left unturned in order to be up to date and fully aware of the requirements for a children's hospice.

From local research it had been determined that there were probably 1,200 families in the North East region who were coping with the most devastating news any parent could hear. Their beloved child would not live to be an adult. Whatever time left was precious and a children's hospice could help make the most of that time, providing expert medical help and professional care but also giving emotional support and practical help.

Kathy wanted to allow the whole family to enjoy the good days and share the bad ones.

The North East had the lowest number of hospice beds for children compared to any other region in the whole country. Some families travelled out of the region which meant day-to-day living, family life and outings were restricted. A number of relationships crumbled under the strain.

The fact that there was a need was not in doubt, but support for her idea for a hospice for terminally-ill children in the north east was essential if her idea were to become reality.

The Strategic Health Authority endorsed the initiative and local MPs also warmly gave their support:
Joyce Quin MP
Stephen Hepburn MP
Chris Mullin MP
Bill Etherington MP

Kathy knew that support for the idea was tremendous. To progress she would need to get down to the practicalities of organisation, planning and fundraising. Little did she realise that her name would be so indelibly linked with the biggest charity appeal in which she had ever been involved - it would take over a major part of her life.

The North East had eight children's hospice beds in Newcastle and four in Billingham. Twelve beds to service an area that ran from Berwick to Teeside and contained the 1,200 families of children who needed them.

It was decided that Sunderland would be the site for the new hospice (midway between the two existing hospices) and so add to the network of care. As with the other hospices, Grace House would benefit children from the whole of the North East.

When other local charities heard of the plans, they were concerned at the affect it may have on their fundraising, but without exception they wished the proposed charity success.

A name for the hospice was required and Grace House was selected as it encompassed the ideals and aims.

"Grace" means "to enhance, to dignify, to enrich".

The Trustees agreed that few names could be more suitable. It encompassed so much of the appeal's mission statement. The parents of a little girl called Grace, (who was suffering from an undiagnosed life-limiting condition) agreed that the hospice could be named after their daughter.

Grace House would be a haven for very sick children, it would be a major source of employment for highly-skilled staff, and would give well-deserved respite for parents.

Kathy was in no doubt, this hospice would be built, she had been meticulous in research. Now she needed money.

On 18th April 2002, a company limited by guarantee was formed in the name Grace House Sunderland. The appeal was launched during National Children's Hospice Week in September 2002.

Registered Charity No: 1100682

At the time of writing this chapter the foundation was firmly established and one day would see a vibrant, efficient and urgently-needed children's hospice in the Wearside area.

A mountain to climb and Kathy was only at base camp

David Hughes

Chapter Three

A Door Is Opened

"David, is it possible to create some Christmas cards that we can sell to raise funds?" The request from Kathy was a good idea except it was October, slightly late to launch cards. However I provided two traditional Christmas cards and it was decided to have a competition among the children at Portland Special Needs School, select their best two designed Christmas cards to be sold in a pack of four on behalf of the Grace House Appeal.

My only contact with children with special needs was the occasional glance when passing a child in a shopping centre or elsewhere, feeling sorry and continuing on my way.

Within a short time the school had selected the two winning cards and I was invited to attend an early morning school assembly where Mr David Blyth, director of Station Taxis was going to present vouchers to the two winning pupils and Christmas selection boxes to the other children. This was a most generous donation from taxi drivers of Sunderland and produced a tremendous amount of pleasure and excitement among the children.

I was escorted into the school and a door opened to reveal a sight that gave me one of the biggest shocks I'd ever had. It took my breath away and to my everlasting shame, I could easily have retreated back outside to my so-called "normal" world.

The assembly hall was full to overflowing with boys and girls of varying ages, all with major problems. To see one child with special needs was sad, to see a small group with tubes, wheelchairs and carers was disturbing. I was now faced with more than a hundred children together in one hall.

The noise was tremendous but no different to any other school assembly and I accepted a seat where I could observe the children and teachers. At the beginning my eyes focused only on the severe disabilities of each child and it was a struggle for me to control my emotions, but slowly it began to dawn on me that no school assembly could have a happier, more vibrant group of children than I was facing. They weren't miserable, disheartened or looking for sympathy because of their problems, they were young children, laughing, talking, arguing, simply being normal. The fact they had a disability was irrelevant to them, they were children who happened to have a problem, didn't want pity and were as much a part of society as me. Each child was an individual living a full life within their capabilities, and their joy to see the presentations was heart-warming.

Afterwards, I had the opportunity to speak to children, teachers and carers. The more I communicated, the closer I became and the more I realised I was in the company of some wonderful, dedicated people. I hadn't realised the time, devotion and love that teachers and carers gave to severely handicapped children. I was amazed at the vitality of the children. No one here wanted pity, they were too busy living.

how I would cope at home because it was as if the hospital had moved into my home. My whole life revolved around the timetable of giving Lee his fifteen different drugs throughout the day.

LEE WITH
CHAMPION BOXERS
BILLY HARDY AND
PRINCE NAZEEM

PARTY TIME WITH FRIENDS

"A Children's Hospice nearby would have been a Godsend."

23

"Without our faith I don't know how we could have survived. It's life that makes you the person you are but our faith has given us the strength to bear the burden. Three times Lee was told by a doctor 'You're going to die' yet he never gave up. We spent birthdays, Christmas and New Year in hospital but when carols were sung I had to retreat into a corridor, sob my heart out, pray, pray and pray.

"Lee came home, no more could be done, the cancer had spread to his stomach and he had developed thrombosis.

"He had rushed into life as if he'd known it would be short, so many people said his life had touched and inspired them. He had a full life in a restricted environment but lived only sixteen years.

"I'm sad but proud to have had my beloved son, Lee.

"The hardest thing was to watch Lee die. When the nurse said he was dying I locked myself in the bathroom and cried to Jesus for help, but I had to let Lee go. I wanted to run away but held him tenderly and wish I could have said more words of comfort but I wasn't strong enough. It's only by God's grace that I cope with his death."

He died on February 13th 2003

LEE COOK: Died of a brain tumour at the age of 16.

Keith was only 14 years old when he wrote the incredible letter printed below. He is autistic and suffers from cerebral palsy.

The Day That Changed My World

LEE
By Keith Cook
His Kid Brother

"My story really begins on a Wednesday night at church youth group. It is a place I always enjoy going to mostly because of the people. This might sound silly but I have known them so long they feel like family. The night was like any other, we sat and listened and learned about God and played some games. The conversation between the youth group that Wednesday was a bit different from other times, instead of being about each other it was about going to see Dependance which is a very good Christian group that goes round different schools and they were holding a concert which we were going to see that Thursday.

"The next day I went to school as always with one thing on my mind and it wasn't politics or what would happen in ten years, no, the only things that I thought about concerned ME. On the way home I couldn't stop myself from telling my taxi driver that I was going to see Dependance and how great they were, I really don't think she cared but being the nice person she is she listened anyway.

"As my taxi pulled up to the house I saw June's car, June is my mam's best friend and in a way is a close friend to me, mainly because of the way she has helped our family. She is also someone very close to me because I spent a lot of time with her when my mam and brother Lee were in hospital. My brother Lee was very ill with a brain tumour he had had for about six years and as you could imagine he was in hospital a lot, so my mam stayed with him while I stayed with my mam's friends and sometimes family in their houses. The funny thing about stopping with so many different people is that you get to see that most people are not that different, ok they look different but most of them live plain and ordinary lives. The hardest part about living with different people in their homes is getting used to their way of living, like some people eat dinner in the dining room on the table; others would eat in front of the TV. Anyway next to June's car was the car of the doctor who had come to visit Lee, which really didn't concern me because at that time we had visitors a lot, mostly doctors to check up on Lee. But as I walked in the door it was different. All I could hear was a cry of pain from Lee's room, so I walked up stairs, not feeling right inside but as I got to the top I turned to the door of Lee's room and saw my mam who smiled at me then June came out of the room and took me to McDonalds, whilst she then explained how ill Lee had been that day.

"As we drove home I had forgotten all about the concert I started to think of more important things. Then we were home. I opened the door and June went in first and with-out any warning, faster than a bolt of lightning, my mam hugged me. At this point she was crying. At first I just thought she has had a really bad day then she said "Sorry" I thought to myself "What is going on?" then June, with tears in her eyes looked at me and said "Lee has died." I didn't believe her. I asked "Died?" and she just nodded.

"I walked up stairs to see him, in the room was the doctor and nurse packing away, then in the corner was Mary who is a Rainbow Trust worker and had become, through three years of knowing her, a close friend to our family. Then I saw Lee's body lying there on the bed I looked once and then started to cry and went down to the fourth stair and just sat there.

"June thought it might be a good idea for me to miss the Dependance concert but I wanted to get out, so she said to go wash the tears away from my eyes. So I went up to the bathroom and washed my face while Mary and mam were ringing the family and friends to tell them what had happened.

"In our bathroom we have a mirror. I would often talk to it if I ever had problems, which I needed to think over. It might sound odd but it helps me work things out, but this time I just stared at myself and then went down stairs.

"We arrived at the concert, I had promised June I wouldn't say anything to the rest of the group until after the night was over. Just before it started my cousin Rachel came in with tears in her eyes and sat beside me. Rachel was on my mam's side of the family and is my closest cousin. She slept over which was pretty cool sometimes but she was one year older and sometimes tried to take control, but I had never seen her so upset. Then she started to cry and went to the back with June. I sat in my seat and didn't really pay much attention to what was happening around me, it was like I was physically there but mentally I was in my own world.

"At the end of the concert June broke the news to the others. I wasn't there next to them but I could see them crying then other people from Lee's school came up to me and started to say sorry which in a weird way makes you feel better about the whole thing, it is comforting to know that some one else feels what you feel. When I arrived home there were a lot of people there but I can't remember all of them just that I went straight to my other big brother Steven who was in the kitchen with my favourite uncle, who is called Ray, who was trying to lighten up the mood by telling jokes. As you could guess it didn't work.

"That night Mooney slept over but it wasn't like any other time. It felt odd, this is because instead of talking about five songs out at the time or our top five films, we just lay there quiet. We didn't even talk about the concert we just lay there, me on the bed, Mooney on the floor. Then it was like someone had switched on a light in my head because things all came together and started to make sense and I started to answer questions in my head like why Lee was ill and started to think of things that really mattered not to me but in general. Then I closed my eyes and asked myself WHAT NOW?

"A few days passed and we had to deal with a funeral but the people from the church helped my mam with some of the arrangements. Over a hundred people turned up from all over. They weren't all family, there were teachers, friends, nurses, doctors and some people he met in hospital.

"It still puzzles me how one person can have such an impact on people's lives. Over the months we have had a charity fund raising for all the charities and the hospital that has helped us. The biggest one was the balloon race where Bob Johnson turned up which was really nice of him. For me and my mam, well at the moment we are coping and are just trying to patch things up.

Sky filled with colour in memory of tumour victim Lee

"However I still haven't found my perfect place and I've stopped trying and that's because there is no perfect place."

***

Keith has produced one of the most moving documents I have ever seen.

Keith and Lee in early days

I switched off my tape recorder.

I'll never forget a brave lady called Diane who had an exceptional son called Lee, and a remarkable boy called Keith.

Chapter Five

June the Angel Lady
June Waterstreet

I was aware that the story would have sad moments and relating the story of Lee, the Bandana Boy was both sad and inspirational, how a boy could be so brave in the face of the inevitable is remarkable. My next visit was to a lady equally as inspirational but in a different way.

So many people believe life is almost over when they become pensioners. The lady who would relate her story proved that a new life can begin at the same time as collecting an old age pension.

A smiling, white-haired pensioner greeted me at the door of her neat bungalow. The house had a warm lived-in atmosphere and her first task was to offer a morning cup of tea.

"So you're The Angel Lady?" I asked. Smiling she replied: "Well it's a good name for what I do and it catches the eye of the reader when the press cover my story."

June was not a pensioner watching television and whiling away her old age. She was a buyer prior to retirement and continues to have a bright sparkle in her eyes, an alert brain and boundless energy. These assets she now utilised for the benefit of the Grace House Children's Hospice Appeal.

Her husband Alan was a quiet, tolerant man who gave her his total support and was a highly skilled photographer. Both June and Alan led extremely busy lives.

It all began when June decided she wanted to do something for children, having seen so many children in hospital at the same time as her granddaughter Kelly. She saw Kathy Secker's press story, phoned her up and offered to help raise funds.

At that stage June had no idea what she could do.

One day, while walking through the local shopping gallery, she stopped at a shop selling small glass angels. With an ex-business and buyer's acumen she said to herself: "That's it, I'll sell angels."

She entered the shop, explained to the owner her intentions and was given the name of his supplier - a firm called Mayflower Glass. With £203.04 of her own money she bought her first carton of small, glass angels. These were sold at £3 each and in only two days she had sold out.

The legend of the Angel Lady had been born, and in two years she had sold angels to the value of £23,000.

She painstakingly packed small angels in white cotton wool and then into a fine cotton bag of various colours finishing the present with a small tag with the words: "Thank you for your support."

Angels on Display

June explained:

"I pack them in cotton wool to depict an angel on a cloud but angels aren't all white, that's why I pack them in different coloured bags."

They were the most delightful small present I'd seen and I could fully understand her incredible success.

June went to craft fairs, schools and churches, anywhere that she was accepted. "I'm 65 years old and will carry on as long as possible." She expanded her glass range to include small bears with wings, birth stones and a special glass bride and groom. She even had a team of friends who sold them on her behalf.

June with Joyce Kinghorn (next door neighbour)

She hadn't retired from business, she's involved as much as ever – this time for children.

June had a clear target, her aim was to sell glass angels to the value of £65,000 to pay for a sensory light room to be installed in Grace House Children's Hospice. One day June saw children in a sensory light room and their little faces convinced June that her glass angels would one day provide such a facility in the new children's hospice.

I was shown into her kitchen that resembled a small warehouse, which proved that glass angels now played a major role in the lives of June and Alan. Not for them the quiet life of pensioners, they were in business with a good product, huge potential market and a clear target. One day, many young children would benefit from the efforts of such dedicated people.

As I was leaving the bungalow, I noticed a basket full of broken glass angels in the hall and June explained that it was inevitable an occasional angel was broken.

"Why do you keep them, they can't be mended?" I asked.

With a twinkle in her eyes, she replied:

"God wouldn't reject anyone not perfect, so I can't throw them out."

Glass bear

Glass angel

David Hughes

Chapter Six

Evie

Nichola and Michael were thrilled at the birth of their daughter, Evie Elizabeth, on September 18th 2002. However they were unaware that their baby had a major problem and within weeks she would need treatment for a dislocatable hip, hernia and pneumonia. Little did they realise that one day they would face an appalling dilemma.

When I called to record the story of Evie, Michael was leaving the house on business but they had decided that Nichola would relay the details of their baby's life.

Nichola took the tape recorder and quietly gave me this very moving story.

"Our lives changed the day Evie was born. Hospital became almost a second home. No sooner had one problem been diagnosed when something else developed resulting in more tests, diagnosis and treatment. I stayed with Evie in hospital, Michael visited almost every day before work.

"We didn't own a car, which was a problem, but support from both families was tremendous.

Evie with mother and father

"Eventually Evie was diagnosed to be suffering from – Mucolipidosis II – she was missing an enzyme in her body that breaks down toxins. Her body was storing toxins that were dangerous.

"She had limited physical movement, couldn't feed herself, had hearing difficulties and major problems with her lungs. We were aware that she would never reach adulthood but she was the most happy, bubbly little girl in the world. We always knew when she wasn't feeling well, she simply stopped smiling. She gave such love and delight, I worshipped her every second I was with her.

"We tried everything, went everywhere to find a cure but to no avail. A support group in Buckinghamshire was a help, particularly when the doctor was from the North East of England, we had an instant rapport because he understood our dialect.

"We made a major decision when Evie needed surgery for her dislocatable hip. We were told it would be dangerous and she would be encased in plaster. She couldn't walk or crawl and would be deprived of her daily bath (she loved being in the water). The doctors agreed with us that Evie had no pain and it would be unfair to subject her to another operation.

"When Evie was in her second year, an operation on her abdomen lasted seven hours. I couldn't sit still and paced the hospital corridors crying and praying for my baby. At that time I was studying for my driving test and must have read the Highway Code at least twenty times. The time passed by and Evie had survived yet another crisis and once again returned home.

"She couldn't sit up unaided, speak or feed herself, but I was determined that somehow her life would be fulfilled. We bought her a little walker aid to sit in and incredibly in a short time she began moving her little legs and was able to move around the room. The fact that she moved backwards didn't matter, we were thrilled.

"I spent hour after hour mouthing words and making signs with the hope that she would copy. One day she said: 'Mama', there aren't sufficient words in the English Dictionary for me to describe my feelings of pride, delight and sheer love for my special girl. She progressed to using her eyes and arms to indicate which toy she wanted to play with or nursery rhyme to hear.

"2004 was the best year, within a seven month period she was only in hospital once. The summer was warm, we spent hours in the garden. As a family we were happy and contented, we even dared hope the predictions on her future prospects may be wrong.

"It had taken Social Services a year to have a hospice in Newcastle accept us for respite and a break from our twenty four hour, seven days a week, non-stop care.

"At the beginning I was apprehensive, the very word hospice indicated blackness and death, but I was so wrong. It was light, happy and full of music. Staff were caring, understanding and the facilities for children were fabulous.

Evie in her walker enjoying life

"One little boy was whirring round in his wheelchair, boasting that his parents were on holiday in Spain but that he preferred to stay with his friends at the hospice. Facilities for families were as good as a hotel, but I only left Evie for a few hours at a time to allow Michael and I the luxury of shopping or going for a meal together. It was a wonderful respite, if only the hospice had been nearer home I know it would have been much better.

They were told that the cerebral palsy would not get worse and would not be so noticeable while Yanina was a baby. The problems would arise as she got older and frustrated at not being able to do all the things she would like to do. Some sufferers overcome such problems but they were warned to prepare for the worse.

Cerebral palsy is a paralysis of the muscles (primary those of the limbs) caused by a brain abnormality. The affected part of the brain is unable to control certain muscles, making them stiff and difficult to use. Even reaching for a toy may be jerky and frustrating.

There was panic and fear when Yanina developed a breathing problem and a tracheotomy was performed (this requires an incision into the trachea).

"To see this in my baby's throat was both frightening and heartbreaking," Marie said, with tears in her eyes.

"Bernice busied herself like a mother hen, fetching, carrying and being helpful to her sister in her way. The special bond between twins was incredible. Bernice showed a sense of love and caring far beyond that expected from one so young. But caring and nursing Yanina was a full-time job and became a way of life," Marie continued. "A small amount of help was given by Social Services, but when Bernice became old enough to bathe unattended, it was withdrawn. Bath time was always a problem, I couldn't put two into the bath, nor could I leave one on her own, everyday was a nightmare."

Respite for Marie came from her sister Irene who provided unstinting support, care and practical help, particularly taking Bernice out into the park for walks. Of course, the twins' grandad had a loving bond; he would sit holding the hand of Yanina, talk and sing without thought of time. The look on her face, smiling at his antics was a joy to see.

"If there had been a children's hospice nearby it would have been wonderful," Marie said, with feeling.

Yanina worshipped a remarkable nursery nurse called Rosemary. There was a close affection between them, and Yanina "was spoilt rotten".

When she got older Bernice went to a nursery school but Yanina went to a special needs nursery. A place was offered to Bernice in the special needs nursery if Marie would sign a form claiming that the fit and well twin also had special needs or had social problems – Marie refused.

As the years went by, Yanina was growing into a remarkable little girl with fortitude far greater than her tender years. She was constantly in and out of hospital, operations, treatments and permanent care, yet never once complained nor showed dissent. Her smile was infectious, her eyes spoke volumes and she enchanted who ever she met. Incredibly, she had the ability to smile and captivate the friendly visitors, but would close her eyes or turn away at those less sympathetic.

Marie recalled with anger those people who would stare at Yanina as if she were a freak.

"I felt like shouting: 'My baby is a normal child who has a problem, why don't you stop staring', I felt so angry and sad for my baby."

Above, Yanina with
Rosemary.

Opposite, with Aunty
Irene and dad John

When Yanina was happy her laughter was a joy to hear, particularly when she was presented with a special needs bicycle. Friends who owned a pub in Benidorm, called the Wooky Hollow, held a charity night and raised £1,800. When taking her out in the park with her cycle, people would stop and be captivated at a little girl with so many problems yet obviously so happy with an inner glow of contentment.

Glyn Bathgate raised £3,282
to buy specialised computer
equipment for Yanina.

Also in the picture is her sister
Bernice.

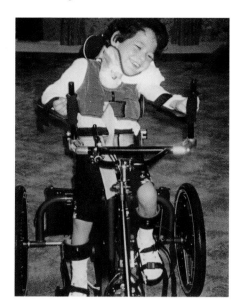

Happy and content with her own special bicycle. She loved being in the park just like other children.

Her time to transfer to Sunningdale Special Needs School was approaching with trepidation. Would she receive love and care? The fears of Marie and John were unfounded, the carers were wonderful, she was given ample love, care and affection and Yanina couldn't wait to attend. During her last two years, a bond was created with Viv and Kevin, her teachers, that was a pleasure to see. They gave her some happy moments that brought such joy into her young life. It helped her to bear her problems with a bigger smile than usual.

Marie ended our conversation with tears in her eyes. "We hoped to have Yanina accepted into Percy Hedley School in Newcastle, which specialised in cerebral palsy. They provide one-to-one care and superior facilities. It was too expensive for our local authority who claimed that Yanina was too disabled."

After a long pause Marie continued.

"One thing that helps to sustain us is the knowledge that Yanina was a lovely, pure, little girl who had never been exposed to one second of evil. In spite of her problems she was an example to so many people with her contented acceptance of her burden – she was a little angel."

From the beginning, Bernice refused to discuss her twin sister Yanina with me. She still suffered traumas following her sister's death. After meeting the family a number of times to finalise the story of Yanina I gained the confidence of Bernice and I was amazed and delighted to receive the following note from her in the post one morning.

> Yanina always laughed when I played with her no matter how rough I was. She never cried when I played with her and dragged her across the floor to my mam's bed. My mam shouted at me but I played with her anyway.
>
> I miss my sister !!!
>   Bernice

Yanina developed major problems and died suddenly at the age of eight on January 31st 2003.

Hundreds of cards and letters testified as evidence that a little girl can touch the hearts of so many people during her brief life.

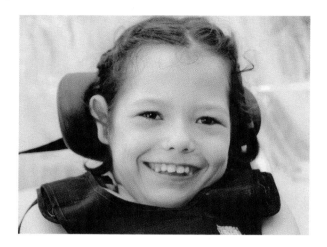

Yanina – "She was a little angel"

"I miss my sister !!!" Bernice

Chapter Eight

Kevin : A Special Teacher

"You must speak to Kevin." "Kevin is an exceptional teacher." "Haven't you interviewed Kevin yet?"

Time and again, his name came up in various conversations, so it was almost by popular acclaim that I made my appointment to meet Kevin at Sunningdale School. "I can give you half an hour," he said.

I only saw the school entrance hall, corridor and a less-than-tiny office. I was greeted by a smiling giant of a man who answered four telephone calls, made two important decisions as we walked to his office, yet he still had time and the courtesy to make me feel welcome.

"I hope I'm not taking up too much of your time?"

"No problem," he replied as we entered his office. After a brief explanation for my visit, I handed over my tape recorder to Kevin. From that moment he took over, I didn't need to ask questions, he talked for half an hour, with brief breaks to answer his telephone.

The recording speaks for itself, the man, the teacher, the warm human being shine through his words.

"I am 51 years old, married with no family of my own, in fact my wife works here at Sunningdale. From an early age I've been with children, my mother was deputy matron at a school in Scotland that had handicapped children, and we often had foster children.

"In 1991 I gained my teacher certificate at Langham Towers in Sunderland and obtained a job at Ford Hall School which catered for special needs children. I was the woodwork teacher for 19-year-olds until 1998 when I arrived here at Sunningdale School where I'm currently the Assistant Headmaster. Ironically my original intention was to be a policeman, because I didn't expect to qualify as a teacher."

Kevin took a brief phone call and continued.

"Did you know that prior to 1972 the special needs children weren't even allowed into school? It was the 1972 Education Act that gave them the right to an education."

"Sunningdale School opened in 1988 for severely and profoundly handicapped children from the age of 3 to 13 years old. We can concentrate better now that the number of children is down from 220 to 75 with ages from 2 to 11 years of age. The children come from all over the city of Sunderland.

"Some of my children have recognised symptoms, i.e. cerebral palsy, Downs syndrome etc, some have rare problems, and others are not diagnosed. Everyone wants a diagnosis, a label on a child, but I believe there is good and bad without a label, because, as long as the child's illness is not known, the medical people keep looking for something positive. Once diagnosed they are put into a category and there they stay (still that's only my personal opinion).

"I enjoy coming to work every day of my life. I never know what to expect, every day is a different challenge. I love every child in this school, they are my children. I am privileged that parents give them into my care. Because they deal with them all the time they are so precious, yet each parent has the trust to put them into my care for a short time.

"When a child dies it's like losing a member of the family. But I firmly believe the family and children benefit from coming to Sunningdale, because we give them a special commodity – tender, loving care."

Kevin stopped to answer another phone call, made an on-the-spot decision then proceeded to make a comment that typifies this remarkable man.

"In my opinion, communication is the most important thing, even more than education, because unless you can communicate you can't educate. The problem isn't as many people assume, that the children can't communicate, they can, even if it's by lifting a finger or with their eyes. The real problem is for me to understand their method of communication and what they're trying to tell me – it's my problem not theirs.

"Every child here is an individual, bright, breezy, with their own personality. They all have problems, with aids and support, but I have a problem and need to wear glasses - it's important to recognise we are all people with problems."

Kevin moved on to a subject that he found hurtful.

"I've recently taken four children to a shopping centre for them to do some Christmas shopping. I understand that it can be a shock to see children in wheelchairs with tubes etc. attached but there are predictable reactions by the public.

> They
> DELIBERATELY CROSS THE STREET TO GET AWAY.
> People are embarrassed when they see a child with severe disability, they don't know what to ask.
> Or
> PAT THE CHILD'S HEAD saying to the carer's "Would Johnny like a drink?" as if the child wasn't there.

I try to encourage people to talk to the children, accept them for what they are. If you took away the wheelchair, oxygen and tubes they are all young people with feelings and personality. It's what people see that is the problem. The worst part of the job is trying to re-educate society in their attitude to disability."

I interrupted his flow because I realised my time was nearly up and I was encroaching on precious minutes of a busy man.

"Kevin, why do you do this job, it's demanding, responsible and highly emotional?"

Without a second thought and with obvious integrity Kevin answered:

"David, a smile, laugh, slight response, interaction with the children and their parents, this is my reward for doing this job. Yes, I need a wage to live, but I get so much love and inspiration from these children it's a privilege to come here every day."

Kevin switched off the tape recorder; I sensed he'd been away from his children long enough. Now I knew why so many people had implored me to speak to Kevin. He was indeed a special person.

Sunningdale School

Following his enlightening interview, Kevin invited me to tour the school, meet the children, teachers and carers. I would make direct contact with the children, try to absorb the atmosphere in the school and obtain yet another aspect of "special children" who have a life-limiting or life-threatening illness.

Sunningdale School existed for children with profound, severe and multiple learning difficulties.

Its brochure quoted ample statistics on statutory assessments, national curriculum programmes and other target figures. I wanted to obtain my own impression of the school activities without my thoughts being influenced by a mass of statistics or league table achievements.

The school was immaculate, spotlessly clean and modern. From entering the main door, it was obvious it was a school for young children, with its posters, colourful walls and bright lighting.

As we walked along the corridor Kevin had a word for everyone, children and adults, greeting them by their first name and knowledgeable of each child's illness and history. Without exception, this remarkable man was greeted with a smile and immediate recognition by everyone.

We visited several rooms to see children of different age groups from three to eleven-year olds. My visit extended over almost three hours and I had the opportunity to observe children and adults at close range.

To quote the individual name of any of the adult teachers and carers would be unfair, because without exception I observed the most dedicated team of people it had been my privilege to meet. I will never forget the young lady, sitting on the floor, patiently nursing a beautiful, little girl, who was crying and couldn't be pacified. Three ladies stroking and gently exercising the little limbs of children unable to move on their own. With flour all over the table, a group were trying to mix a cake, and other children were being dressed to be taken for some fresh air. No children were without attention or stimulation, the school was a hive of activity, yet the adults looked so happy and contented without a sign of stress. The same response from everyone followed my query: "Why do you do such a stressful job?"

"The job is so rewarding, no days are the same and these children are wonderful, we wouldn't dream of returning to a main stream school."

Many of the children had disabilities so severe they couldn't speak, walk or control their body functions. Communication is frequently by eye contact, a smile, scowl or even a grunt. First impression was that these dedicated teachers were simply doing a holding service for young children so severely handicapped their place in society was minimal.

How wrong that first impression!

I sat down to the level of the children, didn't rush from the room, tried to understand the rapport that existed between adult and child and discovered a world of communication that was so wonderful the scene will remain with me for the rest of my life.

The children were communicating as effectively as any so-called "normal" child, because the teachers were sufficiently trained, dedicated and patient to understand how each child communicates. Throughout the school were happy, vibrant young children, this was their normal life, they were enjoying it to the full. I have never been among young people anywhere in my life that equalled the joy and contentment I experienced at Sunningdale School.

The picture would never leave me of the little girl who suddenly lifted her eyes and gave me a wonderful smile. She couldn't speak or move, but her eyes and smile said more than words could ever convey.

A little boy who could only sit in his chair, unable to traditionally communicate, suddenly placed his tiny hand in mine as I moved near him.

As I was leaving one room, a little boy without prompting or assistance gave me a huge smile and hug.

I would recommend anyone spend a few hours at a special needs school, get close to the children, ignore the aids, tubes and wheelchairs and you will discover a world of the most incredible young people you could ever wish to meet.

Before leaving the school I was shown some innovations, all designed to stimulate the children.

At the end of my visit, I fully understood how parents left their beloved children in Sunningdale School with total confidence.

Equally important it was obvious why the children couldn't wait to attend school every morning.

Patricia (Teacher)

After speaking with Kevin, the Deputy Headmaster at the school for children with special needs, I decided to speak to an ordinary teacher to see if it was a teaching job similar to a mainstream school. Was Kevin a one-off, or did his philosophy pervade all who came in contact with the children needing special care.

I met Patricia, a mother of two children. She trained as an infant teacher and taught at a "normal" primary school after college. After her children were born, Patricia returned as a supply teacher at a school of slow learners and special-needs children but she is now with children with life-threatening illness. This extremely articulate lady had the training and experience of children with special needs, I wondered how she would handle children with life-threatening illness. How different was a teacher's approach in such a situation?

"The children are normal, young people, and are treated as such, except they have a problem." Patricia began to explain her role. "The job is very fulfilling, we try to get the best out of the children. They are praised for the slightest thing and we concentrate on communication, which is absolutely essential, sometimes only eye contact can speak volumes.

"I have been on numerous courses in order to handle any situation, courses to be able to identify signs of a child developing a fit, handling oxygen, medication etc.

"There has been so much advancement by the medical profession that many children who would have died at birth are still alive, admittedly with a short life expectancy but we can give them a full life within their capabilities, who knows what miracle development will be available tomorrow? One little girl was only expected to live to three years old, she is now eight years. Every moment of her life is precious, and our job is to help her enjoy these extra years.

"To have a child with life threatening illness is so hard for the parents, and stressful for relationships, that's why we encourage parents to visit the school at any time and enjoy a coffee morning, we need their support and they need to have a trust in our ability to care for their children.

"It's very difficult to be detached, but it's essential at times to stand back, the nursery nurses can become extremely close to the children and be deeply emotional, particularly when a child dies. However, I wouldn't be doing my job if I didn't feel so loving and caring for the children."

Patricia ended her brief interview by saying: "I love the children, I've grown into the job and I love every moment I'm with them."

I parted from Patricia with a feeling that people who teach children with serious illness had that extra dedication and love that gave them the strength to do an extremely demanding job. The quality of life of the children would be so much the poorer, and the burden on parents far greater if thousands of special teachers throughout the country didn't dedicate their lives to a job that wasn't glamorous or popular.

These people were doing more than teaching, they were adding a quality of life that was so precious to these special children.

I decided to include in this chapter, the story of Pauline. She was not a teacher but her contribution to the lives of special children was immense.

Pauline
A Nursery Nurse Who Is Different

At first sight I would have assumed that Pauline had a gentle job in an art or dress shop, maybe a receptionist or administrator. She was petite, attractive with an infectious smile and immediately made herself at home when she visited with her friend Jean to be interviewed about her work.

Her image totally belied the woman.

Her small stature gave no indication that she was an all-action lady, always looking for the next challenge. Among her numerous adventures, she has snorkelled in the Great Barrier Reef (never having snorkelled before) and was planning to walk the length of the Great Wall of China, and she hadn't been to China before.

All this activity to raise funds for charity.

63

If her private life were different, her work as a nursery nurse was unique. She was a Qualified Hospital Play Specialist. Her title made her job sound a lot of fun; in fact, her own description of work was: "We are an all-singing all-dancing team."

However, the nonchalant quip hid the very serious nature of her job.

Children with serious illness needed special, sometimes drastic treatment. Pauline's task was to take their mind off it, stop them thinking of what they have had or likely to face, she called it diversional play.

She had ample experience for the work. She trained at college to be a nursery nurse so from the beginning planned to be with children. She spent 19 years with premature babies prior to her current job, but Pauline said: "These children are special. The nature of my job means that I get very close to them and when a child dies it is so hard to accept."

But no matter how short their life Pauline helped them enjoy part of every day, but showed the serious side of her nature when she said:

"I encourage families to become involved. I want to support them, be brave for them, show compassion, and yes, I sometimes cry with them. I want to be certain that, at the end of the day, I've done my best.

"From these children I've learned to appreciate a lot more. In their short lives they inspire me, because they have maturity and an understanding far beyond their tender years."

Pauline had an outgoing, happy personality but behind this image was a skilled, dedicated nursery nurse who devoted her life to improve the quality of life of some very special children.

Pauline entertaining children

David Hughes

Chapter Nine

Grace Jones

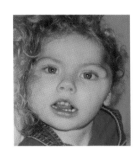

Grace was born on 16th November 1998. Her name means to enhance, to dignify and to enrich. It's doubtful if Debra and husband Darren realised when they selected the name of Grace for their daughter, that, in spite of problems they would face, this tiny little baby would provide enhancement, dignity and enrichment to their own lives far beyond anything they could anticipate on their wedding day.

This may seem a strange introduction to the story of a little girl with a life-threatening illness, but, in all such stories, rarely is it realised the effect on the parents and family who suffer trauma, heartache and constant pressure.

Debra would be the first to agree that her burden is no more nor less than thousands of parents with similar problems. By describing her feelings, actions and determination it may help the reader to realise a child with serious illness is a life-changing experience for the whole family. They are in a different world to a "normal", healthy family; they are outside the formalities of other people with regard to medical, recreational and social involvements.

Debra has a stepson called Dillan; her mother and sister have been a tower of strength and support.

"When Grace was born everything seemed normal, mother and father were ecstatic with happiness," Debra said. "I love my husband passionately but to give birth to a baby is an incredible bond of love that is deeper than I could ever imagine. There was nothing unusual with Grace's birth, but for some reason I had immediate concern." I sat back and allowed her to tell the story of Grace in her words and in her own time.

"I first thought my concern was the normal feeling of a mother, maybe I was being over protective, but within an hour of Grace's birth the midwife took her photograph, the flash made Grace almost jump out of her skin, her arms shot out rigid, which concerned me because I didn't think a new-born could be so affected.

"Grace had a fit later that day, I was terrified, however the midwife said: 'It's just caused by mucus,' and the doctor told me to 'Calm down, it's nothing to worry about.'

GRACE AND DEBRA

"Every second of my life I live and breathe for my baby.

She inspires me to fight the daily battle.

Maybe God will grant her a small miracle."

"With these assurances I was sent home with my beautiful, new baby. No one on earth could feel happier, but I immediately had problems because she wouldn't feed and her little body made continuous jerky movements. After eight agonising days the doctor decided to send my baby for tests at the hospital.

"This was the beginning of my nightmare, I was hysterical and inconsolable, because within minutes of admittance, Grace was suddenly connected to a maze of tubes, oxygen mask and ended up with a fitting on her finger which bleeped every time she stopped breathing, which seemed to occur every few seconds.

"I pleaded for information, but Darren and I were left in isolation, ill with worry. A senior nurse passed by and I pleaded for information, but in a very stern voice she said: 'We're doing all we can, for goodness sake calm down.' I realise it was her way of dealing with a distraught mother but her attitude hurt and continues to trouble me six years later. I was convinced my baby would die, she was so tiny. How could her little body survive these convulsions, I'd never been involved with the medical profession to such an extent, but over the next six years I would get to know some nurses and doctors who were angels and worth their weight in gold, but others who I could only wonder, why did they stay in the medical profession?

"Most of the staff said I was over-reacting and that everything would be all right, but they admitted the cause of Grace's symptoms were unknown.

Grace's dog Chester never left her side while she worked hard with dad's help to make a present for Mother's Day.

Grace in total shock after Santa has been.

They didn't know what was wrong.

"A senior doctor arrived. He was wonderful, caring, understood my worries and said clearly: 'I'm sorry we can't identify the problem, so I'm sending Grace for a brain scan.'

"From then onwards, life revolved around home and hospital, continuous tests, no stable home life until I was finally told they could not identify my baby's problem but one thing was certain, she would be permanently handicapped both physically and mentally, she would be in a wheelchair and could die at a young age.

"That was the lowest point in my whole life and I could so easily have disintegrated, but I was her mother, loved her so much it hurt. Every second of my life I live and breathe Grace. She needed me - little did she know how much I needed her to fight the daily battle with my own sorrow and desperation.

"Darren and I were closer than ever. We made a decision to have no more family; we would get only the best for Grace and give her the best quality of life possible. We took her to Great Ormond Street, specialists in Scotland, Manchester and anywhere we heard of, but to no avail - no one had an answer for her condition. She couldn't feed or do anything for herself, she would scream for half an hour, stop for twenty minutes, scream again on and on. My sister and mother were the only ones I could confidently trust to care for Grace, although a fantastic health visitor from Houghton, called Doreen Lowes, was really special.

"Grace is now six years old, hasn't screamed for two years, rarely cries, she communicates mainly with her eyes, and she can indicate with her mouth when she wants a drink. It is inspirational just to look at her efforts every minute of every day, I feel privileged to be the mother of such a wonderful little girl who is now more content than she has ever been.

"I wanted to keep her all to myself, almost in a cocoon for safety, but I do take her out and accept comments from some people who stare at Grace and say loudly 'God, have you seen that bairn?' They are the ignorant people but so many people comment on her beauty. I can't allow myself to feel hurt or angry, I need every ounce of energy for Grace.

"I believe my darling Grace was born the way she is for a purpose. I'm a Catholic and a believer, Grace was selected to have a children's hospice named after her. She is inspiring hundreds of generous people to raise money, I feel so proud and inspired by my little girl.

No matter how she feels dad can always make her smile

"I dare not think of a time when she will not be here, I think I may just stop the fight myself, but I am hoping to foster children with special needs.

"A desperate decision is looming, she needs metal rods inserted to support her spine, without them she will die. The operation is dangerous but she has lived six years, and I must continue to do all I can. Who knows, God may have decided she has more years of inspiration to provide a hospice called Grace House to be built.

"I believe miracles do happen.

I hope God's listening."

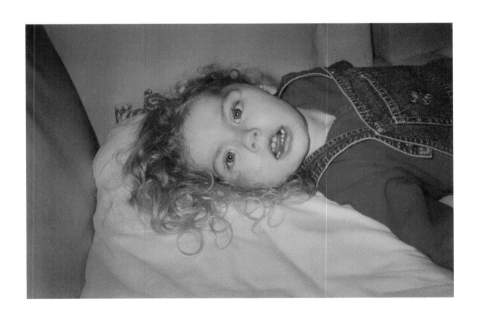

Grace

Mum's plea from the heart

A speech made by Debra Jones at the Grace House Ball at
Ramside Hall on May 20th 2005

"I consider myself to be a very lucky lady. I have a fantastic
husband, Darren, and a family who are such a great support to
us. Most importantly, I have a daughter – Grace, who's so
special in every way that I really do sometimes think she's an
angel sent from heaven to guide me in making positive
changes, not only to my life but to others.

"Lots of families like mine are unfortunate in the way that they
don't have anyone around or anyone strong enough to care for
their child once in a while to give their parents a break.
Providing the chance to have a night away or even just a
night's sleep. It's rare for children with profound disabilities to
sleep through the night. They're often sick, scream or have
seizures. A hospice would offer support for times like these.

"Many mothers like me, to whom I've spoken, have expressed
their desperate need for help and support from a network such
as a hospice that offers respite care. The problem with many
parents is the worry of leaving their cherished loved one so far
away from home. If there was a children's hospice near by
they would be willing to ask for help.

"Grace has profound disabilities. She can't walk, speak, feed
herself, go to the toilet or even scratch her nose if it's itchy.
But amazingly she communicates well with me and her dad.
Her beautiful blue eyes say so much. Because Grace has all
these problems they, unfortunately, create further ones. Due to
her lack of mobility she has recurrent chest infections and
needs major surgery on her limbs. Even without a diagnosis

Chapter Eleven

Xyrelle

A Baby From The Phillippines

Rose and Robert were married, had a baby Xyrelle and lived at Pampanga in the Philippines. Their baby was born on June 14th 2000 and from the first day mother and father were aware that Xyrelle had cerebral palsy and a limited expectation of life.

Rose is a devout Catholic, and when I arrived for an interview, she opened the door of her modest, terraced house with nervous trepidation. We had been acquainted through a senior nurse who was aware of my plan to write a book about "special children". Once Rose was confident of my credentials, a smile on her face appeared, the immediate offer of tea and a comfortable seat made me feel welcome, and ready to record her story.

Although their baby had a major health problem, Rose and Robert decided to build a new life in England, leaving behind in the Philippines, Rose's mother, three brothers and a sister. Finding work wasn't a problem, after all Rose herself is a qualified staff nurse, Robert an assistant chef and they felt that in England there may be some help for their baby.

Mother with baby
Xyrelle at home in
the Philippines prior
to travel to England

The interview was extremely emotional. I was amazed to learn that baby Xyrelle had died only three months earlier. I proposed to stop the interview and return later or even cancel our talk, but Rose was determined to continue saying: "I would feel honoured to have my baby's life story recorded in your book, although she lived only four brief years she was an inspiration to all with whom she came in contact.

"In the first few days of her life it was obvious that my baby had major problems and I silently prayed the Lord would take her to save any suffering, but as time passed my prayer changed to pleading for her to have an extended life. Robert and I decided that no matter how long or short her life, we would give her as full a life as possible. We went on holidays, here in England, gave her our utmost love and care and arranged for her to go to Sunningdale Special Needs School. Of course, she was constantly in and out of hospital.

"Xyrelle could do nothing for herself and needed constant care, so Robert and I decided we would plan our work in order that one of us would always be there; if her life was to be short we would care for our own child exclusively.

Rose and Robert with Xyrelle – Christmas in England

"In return our baby gave us inspiration that will sustain us forever. No matter what her physical problems she had a constant smile and a laugh that was infectious. Her eyes, her facial expression, told us clearly when she was happy, sad or in need. The pleasure on her little face was wonderful to see. Every time she went to school, she loved it and the teachers gave her pure joy in her young life.

"I had a second baby 10 months ago and called her Ryxelle, thankfully she is perfectly healthy, but although my first-born lived only four years the legacy of her happy smiling face will remain with us for the rest of our lives."

On September 3rd 2004, Xyrelle developed a chest infection and suddenly died.

With tears streaming, Rose added her tribute to Xyrelle by saying:

81

"I am proud and privileged to have had such a wonderful baby. The short number of years were filled with a love that was so intense, words couldn't do justice."

I switched off my recorder and said goodbye.

Rose was glowing with pride, recalling the short life of her baby, but throughout my visit she was engulfed in sadness.

Chapter Twelve

Support Unlimited

The title was impressive, Directorate of Child and Family Health (Paediatric Department). The building equalled the title. It was brand new, due to the incredible generosity of Sunderland Footballer Niall Quinn. As I walked into the entrance I was surprised at the atmosphere, no one would believe it was a wing of the Sunderland Royal Hospital. It was more like a children's nursery, ample space, multiple colours, a very light, comfortable waiting room and a receptionist with a genuine, smiling welcome.

I'd arrived to keep an appointment with four nurses who had been recommended by a leading paediatrician, who said: "If you want the real story of special children from a nursing point of view you must speak to Trish and her colleagues." By mutual agreement we'd arranged a meeting on a convenient day and at a time when the team were all together but with a clear proviso – "If an emergency develops the meeting would be postponed."

I was greeted by Trish Maltby; she is a children's community/endoctrine nurse specialist. She led me into a small room to meet her colleagues, Jill McDermot, Lynn Hardy and Christine Hopkinson. Rather than speak to each one individually, we agreed to collectively discuss their involvement with the children. I would record their comments and produce their story for publication.

Trish Maltby (centre) with Jill McDermot and Christine Hopkinson

Each member of the team was highly qualified for the job with an abundance of nursing experience. The four ladies were very articulate and enthusiasm for their job was obvious from the beginning.

They played a massive part in the lives of the children but found it impossible to ignore or fail to be involved with the families. Their contact with the families could be three days a week over many years with the inevitable consequence, they became very close, almost part of the family. They shared the good days, gave support on the stressful days and mourned with the family at a time of bereavement.

The team were in total agreement when comparing life as a nurse on a ward, to their current responsibility. On the ward, they were part of a team of doctors, consultants and other nurses, there was always a second opinion and all the equipment they needed. They could leave the ward at the end of a shift; return the next day, refreshed and aware that the patient had had adequate care.

Going into an individual's home was completely different to work on a ward, with a much greater responsibility. The nurse was on her own, in the environment of patient and family with total responsibility.

They were all agreed that the very first visit to the first patient was traumatic: "Could they transfer all the skills gained on a ward to this one family, could they cope on their own where everything was down to them?" However, that was long ago. I was sitting with nurses who had an abundance of experience caring for children with life-limiting illness.

The aim of the community children's nursing service was to facilitate early hospital discharge for the children whenever possible, prevent admission or ward attendance. Their main workloads was to give support and hands-on nursing care to children with life-threatening illness within the home environment.

These dedicated nurses taught the family to carry out minor treatment for the child but were always on call if anything serious developed and return to hospital was necessary.

The whole team agreed that each child was different with differing needs, and they constantly questioned their nursing approach with such questions:
"Have I done sufficient?"
"Is the family coping?"
"Are they more stressed than normal?"

A community children's nurse specialist, of necessity, must use her own initiative and experience, be aware that available medication is constantly improving and no situation is black or white.

Care didn't end with the sick child, the whole family was affected. Sometimes a child was admitted to hospital for no other reason than the mother was at the end of her tether and needed a brief respite. Other children in the home could feel neglected and contact with other agencies could improve the situation. The nurse became so close to the family, a stint as marriage guidance counsellor was not unknown because the stress on relationships was intense.

Each nurse had approximately 20 serious-illness children plus other minor cases. They could be called out at any time and found it almost impossible to switch off. In spite of their massive work load and responsibility, they all paid tribute and declared admiration for the parents who devoted 24 hours every day, 7 days a week, sometimes over many years to their children.

A comment by Trish Maltby, ending our interview, was a major understatement of their role in caring for children with life-limiting illness. She concluded:

"We all feel good at the end of the day when we've been a small help to the whole family."

My journey would now take me to a young man of remarkable courage.

Chapter Thirteen

Extreme Courage

Alan was 19 years of age; he was very articulate with unwavering eyes and a brain that had produced academic success :

5 GCSEs, RSA Travel & Tourism, A-Level in computers. He was doing a foundation degree course in Computers and Business at Sunderland University.

He was the recipient of numerous achievement awards and was selected to carry the ceremonial baton over one stage in Britain to commemorate the Queen's 50 years celebration.

Throughout the North East, there are people who admired Alan for his bravery, determination and fortitude because he was a nice, friendly young man who had a big problem.

His life was spent in an electric wheelchair, he could move only one hand to direct his chair and control the mouse of his computer. The rest of his body was immobile. For a drink, an item of food and everything else he required he needed assistance. He was totally dependent.

Alan was only 14 years old when he made the decision to have rods fitted in his back to support his spine. Yet another major operation, but the downside of which was loss of control of his head. He had head supports and a multitude of gadgets fitted to his chair to help his quality of life, but he had no control of arms or legs, except slight movement in his hand.

In spite of his enormous disability, Alan was the most positive, thoughtful and caring person you would wish to meet. I sat in amazement during my meeting with Alan and his mother Carol. Throughout the two hours I never heard or detected a note of anger or bitterness at their situation and sympathy was not in their vocabulary.

At the beginning, Carol did most of the talking, although Alan didn't hesitate to contribute. His body may have been of little use to him but he sure could talk. They were so matter of fact in giving me details, it would have been easy to assume we were discussing a stranger. I found it difficult to control my emotions, with Alan explaining the sequence of his life leading up to the remarkable teenager who sat next to me.

Carol and David had been married six years before Alan was born. David was in the merchant navy, Carol was a nursery nurse. She spent two years at sea with her husband prior to the birth.

Alan was a beautiful, blond, curly-haired baby who brought abundant love to the whole family. He was a late starter to walk, but soon developed a good voice. Carol always thought something wasn't quite right, Alan seemed to roll from side to side when beginning to walk, and he frequently fell over, but she was constantly being told, "not to be so fussy", a health visitor even said "it could be flat feet".

Eventually, Alan was sent to hospital for tests and they were told the most devastating news possible - Alan had Duchenne muscular dystrophy, a muscle-wasting problem and he would die.

He was only four years old.

David went to pieces, couldn't stop crying and Carol recalled her devastation at seeing her own father sobbing uncontrollably. She didn't know what to say, she was angry, confused and bewildered at their situation.

The remarkable strength and fortitude of Alan's mother took over. She said with simple candour:

"I realised very quickly that Alan had a problem but it wouldn't be his alone, we are a family, maybe a disabled family, but we will do everything together."

That decision moulded the life of achievement of her son. Weaker parents may not have distilled the character that shines from Alan so brightly today. As a family they came to terms with their problem and simply got on with life.

Eventually, Alan needed calipers for both legs to help him to walk, he used to clomp around but they were a help for him to be "normal". Occasionally, a boy would push him over in the school playground into a puddle, but these episodes were overshadowed by Alan's appearance in a nativity play. There wasn't a dry eye in the house, watching Alan struggle in his calipers to act in the play like the other children.

Carol became pregnant again and was immediately advised to terminate the pregnancy. She and David waited with trepidation the outcome of the tests, but thankfully they would have a second boy called Eion completely free of Alan's problem. With delight Alan announced, "I'm going to have a baby brother", and he couldn't wait to push the pram, calipers and all.

On the day Eion was born, Carol and David were given the shock news that Alan would soon need a wheelchair – he would never walk.

Alan on his bike taking his brother Eion for a walk

The house was adapted. He didn't have the strength to handle a manual wheelchair, so with support from family and friends, £3,000 was paid for an electric wheelchair.

Alan would be in the chair for the rest of his life but he was still only 7 years old.

At the infant school, Alan was given every help and support, in fact, from Carol's viewpoint he was being spoilt with kindness.

He became lazy and expected everything to be done for him because "he was disabled", but she was determined he would live as full and independent a life as he possibly could, and transferred him to a special school at South Shields. It was ideal, Alan was treated as a person and he was encouraged to do everything within his capabilities.

Carol said: "It made Alan accept his disabilities, but so what, I was determined he would realise that he could do some things on his own." This was the making of the teenager who sat with me, independent, positive and alert.

A visit to Disneyland, Paris, 1993 (Alan, 8 years old)

Stresses and strains were inevitable; David had a responsible job on an oilrig, only returning home from Egypt on a monthly basis and taking his share of care the minute he walked into the house. For Carol her only respite was with the help of her mother and carers. Holidays could be very stressful, needing special vehicle ramps, clamps etc. often it would be easier for them to do nothing.

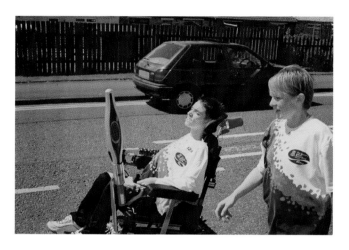

Carrying the baton (Queens Jubilee 2002)

The strength of Alan's mother showed in her final comment: "It would be so easy to sink into apathy and depression and accept that this is our life. It won't get better, but I look at Alan and think, so what, pull yourself together and get on with it."

That was the end of the interview but Alan said he would like to say a few words.

He took over my tape recorder and gave me the most moving yet inspiring interview I have ever heard.

Alan said:

"I have two good friends, Daniel and Mark. They spend time with me, take me out to the pictures or for a meal. We are Sunderland football supporters. In fact, I was once given an award at Newcastle Football Ground, so I wore my Sunderland shirt underneath my jumper, with a bit sticking out.

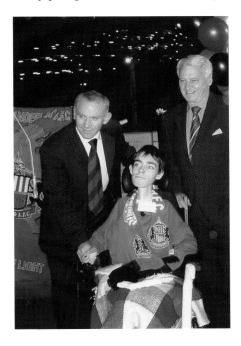

Laying the foundation stone at St Oswald's Children's Hospice
Accompanied by Peter Reid (Manager, Sunderland AFC) and
Sir Bobby Robson (Manager, Newcastle FC)

"Life is quite hard, it's not just what I want. I've got to think of other people, it is difficult when you want to do things and can't. I used to get frustrated, but now I look for alternative ways to get things done. I know it's hard for people caring for me, but it's hard for me to ask.

"I'm proud to be at university, I feel independent, learning like everyone else, just a normal student. This is something I can do on my own, it makes me feel good.

"I've now come to terms with the fact I'm not like a normal teenager but I realise I'm not alone, there are lots of people in the world with big problems. In some ways I am fortunate."

Alan with Mayor & Mayoress receiving Achievement Award

I switched off the tape recorder feeling humble, Alan fully accepted his situation, was neither bitter nor sad. He was living a full life, his family was his strength, and I had the audacity to complain about the bad weather.

"However, family life must be normal, at no time will we upset Daniel or Sophie. They are far too young to realise the long term implications of Daniel's problem.

"The only visual sign is the slight roll in Daniel's walk, other than that he is a normal, loving boy.

"Sophie keeps us all going, she is such a bright happy and loving little girl who does Daniel a world of good, holds his hand at a step, protecting him in her way and thankfully is free from Daniel's problem."

Ian and Susan were only too aware that Daniel's treatment was not a cure, at best it was slowing the inevitable progress of his complaint, however it was not long ago that a boy with a condition similar to Daniel's would have already been in a wheelchair. Even the forecast four years ago that Daniels life expectancy was to his late teens had been extended an extra ten years. Who knew what developments would be produced in the next few years.

The key to the problem was down to research and this was dependant on funding. With so many demands on central government, research for Duchenne muscular dystrophy was under-funded. If research could help Daniel, then Ian and Susan decided to get involved in fundraising. Teaching on a part-time basis, Susan was able to become fully involved, and in the process changed her life more dramatically than she could ever have imagined.

Susan was an attractive, slim and very articulate lady, who, prior to Daniel's diagnosis led a quiet life, happy within the bounds of her family, would never have dreamed of becoming involved with, or rocking the boat of any establishment.

Members of Parliament were remote figures in London, consultants were on a pedestal too high to be questioned. In her quest for answers and funding, Susan developed contact with families facing the same problem, joined an internet support group and stood up at her local church and asked for support, something she would never have dreamed of doing.

Daniel with his mother Susan.

Susan embarked on a life of campaigning and fundraising determined to find funding to provide research for Duchenne muscular dystrophy

She was invited to support a lobby campaign to persuade the government to allocate more money to the research and recalled vividly the scene when she and Ian first approached their local Member of Parliament.

"Armed with a photograph of Daniel and signed letters from the public, we went to the local church hall to see our MP. A new experience, we were both feeling nervous and apprehensive as we shuffled along the bench seats until it was our turn to be seen.

"Well, what's your problem or are you here to complain about something?' was the MPs opening comment, however he listened intently to our request and agreed to support us."

They now had the support of forty MPs. The efforts of the group was so effective, a phone call from the Department of Health pleaded:

> We know all about Duchenne muscular dystrophy!
> We know you want money for research!
> We know why the research is vital!
> But please stop sending letters!

The group responded by sending more and more letters with the result that from a recent allocation of £3m given to research by the government, £1.6m of this was given to research for Duchenne muscular dystrophy.

For Susan, life could never be the same. She was now a trustee for a supporting charity and on speaking terms with Lords, MPs and Mayors, people she had never dreamed of, but Susan said:

"I really believe this was all meant to be. God has given me the strength to handle this, it's impossible for me to sit still and do nothing."

She concluded our interview with a comment of sad realism:

"I'm only too aware that everything we are doing may not be for my Daniel, but it will be for others coming behind. It's not a question of **if a cure can be found but when!!**"

I ended our interview; well aware I'd spent two hours with a mother who was determined to leave no stone unturned in her quest for a solution to save lives.

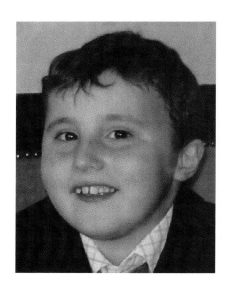

Daniel

A bright and breezy boy with a family who were fighting for funds to aid research in finding a cure for his complaint of Duchenne muscular dystrophy

Chapter Sixteen

Enduring Devotion

Part of life is the creation of memories, particularly memories of children. The first word spoken, first steps, party dress, boyfriend, marriage, holding a grandchild, joy upon joy. Such memories give a purpose to life but are often taken for granted as if it were our right.

Some parents will never have the pleasure of these memories. The life of their child will be different and limited in years but their memories will be no less pleasurable or enduring.

The story of the Wheeler family is a story of love and devotion that is no more than any of the families recorded in this book. They would not claim to be otherwise nor would they expect pity or sympathy, but after spending two hours with David and Diane I feel confident you would wish to read their story.

Sarah with proud mum and dad before diagnosis

I had never heard of a condition called Krabbes – Leucodystrophy.

Krabbes is a genetic disease only transferred by mother or father and is not determined by gender. The disease does not allow proper nerve development in the brain. Every nerve in the body is covered by a myelin sheath which carries the electrical impulses to every other nerve. In Krabbe, this sheath is not forming correctly; consequently proper messages are unable to be carried to other nerves.

Children with this devastating and rapidly progressive disease eventually lose all mental and movement function, become deaf and blind and usually do not survive beyond two years of age.

There is no cure, but if diagnosed at birth a bone marrow or umbilical cord blood transplant is possible, but usually by the time symptoms are present it is too late. Most of the children die of pneumonia as a result of a weakened immune system.

For David and Diane Wheeler they described life as a "permanent living bereavement", waiting for the day their beloved daughter Sarah would succumb to Krabbes Leucodystrophy.

Sarah was eight years old and they believed she was the oldest survivor of the disease in Great Britain.

She was diagnosed at the age of eighteen months and had an expectation of only two years of life. Her life was spent lying on her back, she was blind, couldn't speak or feed herself. Her means of communication was her smile or a slight movement in her hands if she were unhappy.

Sarah with mum and grandmother

For six years her father and mother have endured a regime of care that could only be accepted because of their intense love and devotion for Sarah.

Their day began with a half-hour of chest massage to clear her lungs. She was given food and medication through tubes and taken to Sunningdale School at 9am until 3pm, but her mother couldn't bear to have her out of sight, consequently she spent the day at school helping to care for Sarah and other children.

Sarah adored this special school where stimulation and attention produced a happy, tired little girl on her return home.

Her sister Toni, was a seventeen-year-old, healthy teenager. Two rabbits, a fish and a Jack Russell dog complete a family that was permanently committed to the welfare and quality of life for a little girl who was unable to join in their activities.

107

Sarah with sister Toni

At bed time, mother Diane slept on a camp bed next to her daughter's bed in case of emergency. <u>This routine had prevailed every day and night for six years.</u>

David said: "We brought Sarah into the world and we will care for her as long as necessary. She is such a lovely girl, I'm convinced she has been sent to us for a reason."

Sarah had certainly brought the meaning of unconditional love to the Wheeler family; Diane said: "When my little girl dies it will be a nightmare."

Every morning was a bonus to see Sarah alive and awake, for six years they'd endured this alarming experience and would be delighted for it to continue for many years to come.

Sarah was a beautiful little girl who seemed determined to survive to enjoy the enduring devotion of her family.

Chapter Seventeen

Matthew

Paula and Colin were married on Friday, 13th February 1998 with the same aspirations and expectations of all young married couples. Their first child, Matthew, was born seven weeks premature and although a small baby, he seemed to be a healthy, happy child. Within days he developed an infection, his heart rate dropped, needed oxygen and his kidneys weren't functioning properly.

The shock to this young couple was tremendous, they could see him deteriorating, he was sedated and due to his kidney malfunction his little body was swollen and his weight doubled.

Remarkably Matthew survived, his kidneys began to function and he was getting better but Paula and Colin were concerned because they knew that Matthew wasn't developing as he should.

When Matthew reached the age of six months he was diagnosed with cerebral palsy and Paula was inconsolable. She blamed herself, wished she hadn't borne her baby and even found it difficult to look at or even touch Matthew. Colin took over the care of the baby until Paula came to terms with the devastating news, and resumed the role of a loving mother.

All the dreams of the young couple went out the window, they read leaflets, books anything in order to understand the condition. They checked Matthew's progress compared to other children and knew he had a problem.

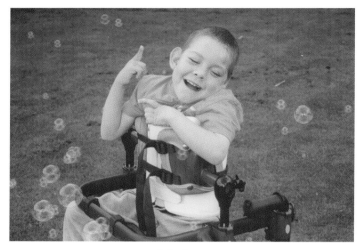

Matthew

They developed a routine of physiotherapy for Matthew and the support from family helped them survive the first few months.

Paula's father was devastated and her mother still feels guilty believing she may have passed on an infection by holding Matthew too close when he was born.

I believe the following decisions of Paula and Colin elevate them into being a special couple, who at a relatively young age decided their lives would embrace a whole family and yet allow them to pursue individual interests and careers. They would be the ideal all round family and Matthew would be an integral part of their plans.

Paula felt cheated that she'd been deprived of a healthy child; they were told that Matthew's condition was not genetic so they decided to have two more children.

Jack was born 19 months after Matthew and Cameron was born four years after Matthew.

Their logic for creating a family of three children was so simple – they didn't want Matthew to grow up as an only child, it would be good for him to have brothers.

Better for Jack, the middle child, to be brought up with a healthy brother on one side and a disabled brother on the other. They would all grow as a family. For Paula and Colin they would not allow Matthew's disability stop their family life and they felt certain that Matthew would benefit from being part of a large family.

A Contented Family

111

The second decision of the remarkable couple was made when Matthew reached the age of five. They reversed roles because Matthew was now too heavy for Paula to handle all day on her own and both Colin and Paula had career ambitions.

Colin was an accomplished artist and writer, by being at home with Matthew, he would have the time and facility to pursue his ambition to be a published author.

Paula wished to become a qualified children's nurse and enrolled at university hoping to qualify in 2007. Since Matthew was born she had seen good and bad nurses and was aware the impact a good nurse could have on the child, consequently with her practical experience and academic qualification, Paula firmly believed she could help other families, give something back and make people aware that having a disabled child isn't all doom and gloom.

First impressions of this remarkable family was that they have a fun house, although they each pursue a career, they work as a team and the children came first.

Paula said: "It was our decision to have children, it's our responsibility, and our time will come when they have grown up."

With the support of a carer, Paula and Colin are able to go out together for two hours once a fortnight, but they are a totally contented couple. The house is noisy and incredibly happy. They are careful to give each child equal attention, help with reading, homework and cuddles. The two healthy children go to bed first and with Matthew being the eldest he receives their undivided attention until his bed time.

Paula and Colin ensure they have their time together by staying up late after the children have gone to bed. Describing their relationship in the face of such frantic activity Colin said: "Paula and I are very close with a strong bond between us, we talk a lot, have the same aims and are completely honest with each other. Having the other two children stops us being obsessed with Matthew's disability and gives us a sense of normality."

Paula ended the story with a brief comment about Matthew: "Matthew has given me something I would not have had. I'm now a part of a world of disabled children I didn't know existed. He's made me realise what's really important in life and we are determined to make the most of what time we have with him. I've wanted to ask about his life expectancy but can't bear to hear the reply. Matthew has such wonderful qualities that others have not, he has given Colin and I such a lot of love we are so proud of our three sons, but you know, we are just a run of the mill family – we're nothing special."

Chapter Eighteen

Abigail

Throughout my journey of discovery into the lives of children with life-threatening illness, I have been in awe of the strength and resilience of children of all ages who accept disability and major medical treatment, yet bounce back to life time and time again.

All children are special, but an extra dimension seemed to develop within a child with a major disability. Their love seemed to engulf family and friends, their fortitude was an inspiration and the acceptance of their situation was a humbling example to many people.

Abigail was a little girl who had endured so much in her young life and continued to bounce back. Her bravery had inspired family and friends, she was the perfect example of a special child.

She was three and a half years old and has already been the subject of front page news in the local newspaper with the headlines:

"Baby Back From The Brink Of Death."
"Little Miracle Abigail."
"She's Defied All The Odds."

Abigail was born eleven weeks premature, was only 3lb 1oz and doctors didn't expect her to survive. Three days after the birth on September 11th 2001, the day of the Twin Towers disaster in New York, Abigail suffered a collapsed lung and a brain haemorrhage. Prospects for this tiny baby were so bleak her father and mother, Philip and Allison, where advised to have their baby baptised.

She was transferred to Newcastle Infirmary, placed in a special baby unit and monitored round the clock. Medical experts worked frantically to develop her little lungs but the haemorrhage had created a build up of fluid on her brain and one week prior to her first Christmas she underwent an operation to drain the fluid. Within a month another major operation was needed on her scull, however this tiny tot had ingredients that were essential for her survival, she had a fighting spirit and the shear will to live.

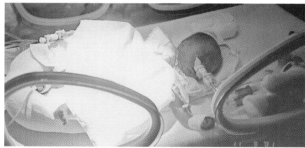

Abigail in intensive care

When I called to record her story the sun was shining, it was warm and Abigail was quietly sitting in the garden playing with her toys. No one could have guessed the trauma she had endured.

Allison and Philip were a happy, friendly couple who were happy to have Abigail's story in my book. Their family comprises: Craig, ten years old and Melissa, thirteen years old, at the time of writing, both from Allison's previous marriage. In addition they had Imogen who was one year old on the day I visited.

Imogen

Latest addition to the family, one year old.

Abigail was born before Allison and Philip were married, it was Philip's first child and he described his feelings at the time of her birth: "Expecting our child to be born was wonderful, we waited patiently for the day to dawn, the first three days of our baby's life was traumatic enough, but on the third day were told to have her baptised because she had cerebral palsy and may not survive. She was my first child, we'd had no warning, the news was like a bolt of lightening and I almost collapsed with the shock. It didn't sink in that her little life was in danger. Allison and I thought it couldn't happen to us, it must be a mistake."

However, it was no mistake, their lives would never be the same. For three months Abigail seemed to belong to the hospital she was in and out so often, but they were in awe at the skill and dedication of doctors and nurses who pulled

Abigail back from the brink to become a loving member of the family.

Her cerebral palsy affected Abigail much more physically than mentally and already she had developed into a child with a determined character. She was a loveable but stubborn little girl who only did the things she wanted to do. She forced her hands to move and even massaged her own weak hand in order to get some movement. It's incredible to see her force her little body to do the things she wanted to do.

As Abigail got older it was a desire of her parents that she got mainstream education like other children, but they soon realised that she would do better at a special needs school and receive almost one-to-one care and an abundance of stimulation. They accepted the need to organise only what was best for Abigail rather than what they would have liked for her.

This remarkable little girl had an eventful first few years of her life and with medical skill, family devotion and her own will to live, her future was more optimistic than was forecast on the day she was born.

However this story was not only about Abigail but the effect her life had on the whole family and friends.

Abigail surrounded by family

For Allison, it was particularly hectic because Philip was a police sergeant with a stressful job. He was a shift worker and there were times when she coped with the children on her own. Abigail was a full time job, in addition baby Imogen needed constant attention. The older children, Melissa and Craig adored the babies and Melissa, in particular, had matured since the birth of Abigail. She had developed into a lovely young woman and was a huge help to her mother. When Allison found the stress too difficult to cope with, her mum, dad, aunties and uncles could always be relied upon for support.

Philip could be called upon to face stress at any time in his job as a policeman, but having to care for Abigail had been an experience that had changed his attitude to life. He took one day at a time and although they had some testing times his love and bond with Allison grew stronger due to their joint caring for their children. Philip found himself impatient with those people who constantly complained about trivialities in life. For twelve years he had taken part in the Great North Run, raising money for charity, but with family responsibilities his training was reduced to a daily four mile run to work, donned a uniform and began duty.

Allison and Philip's day began at 7am and didn't end before 10pm. Shopping was often done at 7:30am at the local supermarket. Their respite was on a Saturday evening out with friends. The children were safe and well cared for and that one evening out helped both of them wind down and prepare for the following week.

They had bought a caravan which allowed the whole family to get away for an occasional holiday without the trauma of staying at hotels and away from people who stared at Abigail.

Allison gave two brief stories that she would like to be included:

"When it seemed that we may lose Abigail when she was born, I tried to gently explain to Melissa and Craig that we 'may lose their new baby sister', with such innocence Craig said, 'don't worry mam, we'll soon find her again'."

They didn't lose Abigail, Craig gained a new sister whom he worshipped.

The next story was the conclusion of Abigail's story.   It typifies how a disabled child could create a love so strong that a whole family would be fulfilled.

Allison and Philip were married on 25th August 2002. Craig and Melissa were proud to be with their mother on her special day.   They longed to have had baby Abigail with them to complete the family but she had been poorly and Philip went off to church on his own little knowing the surprise Allison had in store.

Abigail was well enough to attend the wedding and to Philip's total amazement not only did his bride turn up at the church but rather than carry a bouquet of flowers, she held Abigail. This was his complete family.   Abigail was their daughter who would grow up to love and be loved within a wonderful family.

A surprise for Philip

Abigail at play

Melissa caring for Abigail

David Hughes

Chapter Nineteen

A Children's Hospice

My first image of any hospice was of a place of doom and despondency. A hospice for children was too traumatic for me to even contemplate.

I decided to speak to parents and children who had used hospice facilities in various parts of the country to get their impression, in order to provide a composite image of a children's hospice.

My first impression was totally wrong.

A children's hospice was a place for life, <u>not</u> death. Inevitably, there were sad times, but the following quote seemed to typify the whole philosophy of a hospice.

"We cannot add days to their life but we can put life into their days."

It was a place of warmth, love and caring with staff totally dedicated to obtaining the trust of parents and the unconditional friendship of children. They were all individuals with needs and desires that were catered for to an extraordinary extent.

To many of the older children it was a holiday, "a time to be away from mum and dad". Parents needed a rest from 24 hours' caring, and the break in a friendly environment was equally as refreshing for the children.

Every facility was available to help the children enjoy the break, toys, computers, art, TV and even Jacuzzis. Often quoted was the comment: "We get freedom of choice, even deciding what time to go to bed."

It wasn't easy for parents to hand over their loved ones to a strange carer. They felt responsible for their own child and reluctant to be out of sight for one second. However, every effort was made to gain the trust of parents.

Accommodation was provided for whole families to enjoy a brief stay until they were confident the love and care the children receive met their requirements. Within a short time, families were satisfied, children were delighted and the whole family enjoyed a well-deserved respite.

Many of the parents interviewed claimed that without the respite offered by a hospice, they would have found it very difficult to cope 24 hours a day, year after year after year.

Support wasn't confined to hospice stay alone. Even after returning home contact was constant to ensure the families knew there was always someone available to give advice and help. Once contact had been made with a children's hospice the families would never be allowed to feel alone with their problem.

My image of a children's hospice had changed from one of doom and gloom to a facility that provided love, care and enjoyment of life.

David Hughes

Chapter Twenty

Gordon McClurg

Pure Inspiration

It would be wrong to call Gordon "a special child", because he was 26 years of age. I've decided to end my journey with his story because it seems to encompass everything this book portrays. Every story I've recorded is an example of a child's courage, a parent's dedication, a carer's support or a teacher's inspiration.

Ending my book with Gordon's story seemed to be a fitting summary and emphasised how a determined family could move mountains, achieve the impossible and provide an example from which other families might benefit in years to come.

Marion and Norvil met in 1969 and married in 1974. They lived in Belfast in the midst of the troubles. Eventually, they were blessed with three sons, Graeme, Gordon and Stuart.

Stuart, Gordon and Graeme

There was a two-year age difference between Gordon and his older brother Graeme. They were both healthy and normal boys until Gordon reached the age of two years old. His parents realised that he walked badly compared to his brother Graeme. Their doctor declared they shouldn't worry "it was only puppy fat", even x-ray examination revealed that Gordon only had flat feet. After a year there was no improvement in Gordon's condition, a consultant said: "There was no problem."

It was at this point that Marion and Norvil McClurg took a decision that would lead to their crusade in ensuring their son would receive only the best.

They demanded a second opinion.

After a detailed examination they were given the devastating news that Gordon had 'Duchenne muscular dystrophy', he would be in a wheelchair by the age of ten years old and life expectancy would be no more than sixteen, maximum twenty years.

Gordon was only three years old!

For the next few years Gordon was as normal as possible, went to mainstream school, joined in all activities and, except for the occasional tumble when he needed assistance, he was no different to other children in his class.

His parents were determined that the family would live as normal a life as possible, even to the extent of moving to Scotland to be away from the troubles in Belfast. A scare occurred when Marion became pregnant with her youngest son, Stuart. Blood test and other screenings concluded that the baby was healthy, however even if the tests had proved otherwise, their Christian beliefs wouldn't have allowed a termination.

After five years the family moved to the tiny village of Dalston in Northumberland where Norvil had secured a good job after being made redundant.

It was ideal village life for the whole family, but Gordon's condition had steadily deteriorated, from a period of wearing callipers, constant physiotherapy to a manual wheelchair, until the inevitable electric wheelchair. To Gordon, however, this was freedom, no longer needing help, he could now whiz around the playground on his own.

In spite of his disability Gordon had an abundance of energy, his parents were determined that he would have all the joys of any young boy, a wheelchair would not be allowed to be an excuse for inactivity. Gordon joined the cubs, took piano lessons, went horse riding (with a special saddle) and joined in everything, often with help from his brothers. In addition, his school results were high: his body may have been impaired but he had a good brain.

Gordon with his brother Graeme in Scotland

Gordon horse riding in Scotland

In such circumstances, the strain on relationships is tremendous but Marion and Norvil were both of the same mind, didn't wallow in self pity, determined the family would lead a normal life and were there for each other. They claimed that Gordon had brought them even closer and strengthened their Christian belief.

Eventually, Gordon had to abandon horse riding, piano lessons and other activities, and he decided to have a life-saving back operation when he was only thirteen years old, steel rods were inserted to support his spine. Incredibly, he then embarked on voluntary work for a stroke club, and co-operated with a lady in developing a special horse-drawn carriage for disabled children in wheelchairs. They set up a registered charity called Magic Trust that was still going strong ten years later with three carriages and four horses.

Norvil's work necessitated the family moving to Newcastle and Gordon's disability required a rethink concerning his activities. At 16 years of age many of his previous hobbies were now beyond his physical ability but at no time was the option of succumbing to a wheelchair and doing nothing ever considered.

A new phase of his remarkable life emerged. Gordon joined Rotaract (the youth division of the Rotary movement). He attended conferences, dinners, holidays and even became President of his own club.

Throughout all the activity his education wasn't neglected. On the contrary, he was so successful he qualified for Northumbria University to do a degree course in business studies. This was a major turning point in the life of a young man who was so disabled he couldn't even scratch his own face.

However, the past achievements of Gordon McClurg would pale into insignificance compared to his future activities.

The philosophy of Gordon's parents had always played a major part in the development of their remarkable son.

Marion and Norvil had a strong faith and Christian belief, Norville said: "All life is a gift from God. Gordon may be impaired but he is all the more precious. He enriches our lives, the family, and everyone with whom he comes in contact. We are so fortunate."

He continued: "We were devastated by the diagnosis and struggled to come to terms with the implications of how it would impact on our family life."

Gordon abseiling in Keswick

But their decisions that followed this diagnosis created an amazing young man.

131

They would truthfully explain everything that would happen to him: keep him in a family environment, not treat him as a special invalid; maintain close links with all the extended family; help him understand the management of his complaint and accept there was no cure.

"We didn't help Gordon to cope with his condition, he helped us. That has been the thread all the way through."

"Mum, dad, I want to talk to you. I know you're going to be unhappy, and I expect you to say no."

Gordon and his mother and father were on their return journey from a holiday in Berlin, Germany. This holiday had been organised and planned by Gordon as a thank-you to his parents for all they had done for him, in particular, the holiday was a celebration for his amazing success at university. He had obtained a 2:1 (Hons) Degree in business studies.

With trepidation they waited for Gordon to continue. They had always encouraged him to try anything and were rarely surprised at his activities, but this was different. His tone of voice, the timing and serious expression indicated that Gordon had a major surprise in store - they weren't disappointed.

"I want to get my own apartment, be independent and plan my own life."
Marion and Norvil were silent, but their minds were in a whirl. He had already spent four years in a specially-designed flat at university, was now accustomed to a degree of independence, and had successfully negotiated an academic life of lectures and student activities, but total independence?

"At school other children had seen a TV programme about my condition and began saying that I wouldn't live as long as them. I asked my parents, is it true? Mum told me the truth, I found it hard to cope with!!

"I eventually accepted my fate, realised there was nothing I could do about it and decided to do as much as I could with what time I had.

"I was determined to be as independent as possible. I go to the theatre, holiday in Berlin, Spain and other countries and I'm a member of Rotary in Tyneside.

"I'm grateful to my family, carers and everyone who helps me. I'm really very fortunate and content with my life. I would like to help others with the same condition as myself for as long as God determines."

I switched of my tape recorder for the last time. This was a fitting end to my journey.

David Hughes

"Please help me build Grace House Children's Hospice"

KATHY SECKER

A MUCH NEEDED HOSPICE FOR VERY SPECIAL CHILDREN

EXCLUSIVE GREETINGS CARDS BY 'DAVID HUGHES'
only £1.99 per pack of 4 cards

Have Your Named Brick Built into 'GRACE HOUSE' FREE OF CHARGE !!!
Simply sell 100 packs of cards
Name A Loved One, Group or Organisation

Telephone: (0191) 5166302
or
email: gracehouse@bicne.co.uk

David Hughes   Author/Artist
Retired Co-op Executive, author of four books and an award winning watercolour artist, has designed Four Greetings Cards, Exclusive for GRACE HOUSE CHILDREN's HOSPICE APPEAL.

Please complete the form overleaf and post it to:- GRACE HOUSE CHILDREN's HOSPICE APPEAL, Suite P1, Business and Innovation Centre Ltd, Wearfield Sunderland Enterprise Park East, Sunderland, SR5 2TA

Your Name and Contact Details

Name *(block capitals please)*

. . . .

Address

. . . .

. . . .

Postcode . . . .

Tel: . . . .

Signed . . . .

Date . . . .

ORDER FORM - please send this coupon to
GRACE HOUSE CHILDREN's HOSPICE APPEAL
I will sell 100 packs of greetings cards @ £1.99 per pack = £1

Details for inscription on Named Brick:
(2 lines with up to 10 characters on each line)

Donation Form

Please remember that all your donations count. Whether your gift is great or small your generosity will help us raise the money needed to build Grace House. **Many, many thanks** to you all for your ongoing support.

If you would like to make a donation to the Grace House Appeal, please complete the following:

Name: Mr/Mrs/Miss/Ms ....

Address ....

....

.....................Postcode ....

I enclose a donation of £:

Please debit my Mastercard/Visa/Switch/Solo account for the sum of £

☐☐☐☐☐☐☐☐☐☐☐☐☐☐☐☐ A/c No
☐

Expiry Date on Card ....Signature ....

Card Valid From ....Issue Number ....

IF YOU ARE IN A TAX PAYING SITUATION YOUR DONATION(S) COULD BE WORTH APPROX 28% MORE. ALL YOU HAVE TO DO IS SIGN AND DATE THE FOLLOWING DECLARATION -

Please accept any donation I may make to Grace House under the 'New Gift Aid' scheme.

I confirm that I am a UK taxpayer and the amount of tax I pay does exceed the amount I would like Grace House to claim.

Signature ....

Date ....

Please remember to sign the above otherwise we will not be able to reclaim the tax!

Please return this form to:
Grace House Children's Hospice Appeal
Business & Innovation Centre Ltd.
Wearfield,
Sunderland Enterprise Park East,
Sunderland SR5 2TA
Telephone 0191 5166302
Charity Number 1100682

David Hughes